Why
Children
Matter

Why Children Matter

Johann Christoph Arnold

The Plough Publishing House

Published by The Plough Publishing House
Rifton, New York
Robertsbridge, England
www.plough.com

ISBN: 978-0-87486-884-5
First Printing: April 2012, 2000
Second Printing: April 2012, 16,200
Third Printing: April 2012, 10,000
Fourth Printing: May 2012, 15,000

Cover photos: © Community Playthings

Library of Congress Cataloging-in-Publication Data

Arnold, Johann Christoph, 1940-
  Why children matter / J. Christoph Arnold.
    p. cm.
  ISBN 978-0-87486-884-5
  1. Child rearing--Religious aspects. 2. Children--
Religious aspects-- Christianity. I. Title.
  HQ769.3.A75 2012
  248.8'45--dc23

                        2012009577

Printed in the USA

Dedicated to all the children of the world.

The author and his wife, Verena, with their granddaughter
Stephanie Jean Rimes (September 3 – October 5, 2008)

Contents

A Note to the Reader

from Timothy Michael Cardinal Dolan
Archbishop of New York

Dear Reader,

Since God's commandment to our first parents to be fruitful and multiply, and continuing with unbroken teaching over the course of thousands of years, marriage and procreation have been revealed as not merely an arbitrary precept of God, but as an imitation of his very nature – life-giving love.

In an age where both the importance and definition of family seem to be under constant attack from all sides, my friend Johann Christoph Arnold provides a much-needed perspective on marriage and an approach to child rearing that is at once time-tested and completely up-to-date, and solidly grounded in faith.

In this engaging work, Pastor Arnold explains with certainty that we can still raise children the right way and avoid caving in to the pressures of a confused culture. He doesn't mince words, but his teachings maintain the compassion of the gospel as he genuinely shows his concern for the plight of parents faced with a difficult teenager or a disabled child. As the fabric of family, and society, is challenged, he offers up concrete steps to bolster and encourage those parents who want to pass on to their children the values their parents gave them.

I have often said that the greatest blessing I ever received was being the son of Robert and Shirley Dolan, and being raised within the loving family of my parents and four brothers and sisters. As I read *Why Children Matter,* I found myself nodding in agreement as the love and wisdom of my own parents was reflected in Arnold's sage advice.

In the following pages I invite you to enjoy insights which reflect the experience and tradition of an entire generation of pastors and teachers who guided schools, parents, and children – over the last hundred years – in Europe, South America, and the United States. And I pray that *Why Children Matter* will help contribute to a better understanding of the amazing gift of marriage and family.

Faithfully,
Timothy Michael Cardinal Dolan
Archbishop of New York
New York City, March 2012

Introduction

IN THE FIFTEEN YEARS since I wrote my first book on
child rearing, the state of our children has changed only
for the worse; the world is in crisis because we do not
love our children enough.

God has been just about completely pushed out of
schools and other public places. In many districts sex
education is mandatory right down to the first grade,
and because of divorce and remarriage, cohabitation,
and same-sex unions, the word "family" is used for
almost everything. As a result the true meaning of
Christian marriage – and thus the true picture of the
family – has been blurred, if not destroyed. The tragic
results can be seen everywhere.

Deep down we all long for the family as God created
it, and it is this God-given family order that can bring
stability back to our culture and our children. Sadly,
we often do not want to submit to God's plan, and are

instead distracted by lofty educational ambitions. There is tremendous pressure to turn children into miniature adults.

All of us were created in the image of God, but children are unique because they most closely mirror God's original creation. Returning to that first creation is going to be a tough battle, but it is my hope that this book will give both vision and courage to parents, grandparents, and educators along the way.

When God created Adam and Eve, he gave them – and us – the commandment to be fruitful and multiply and by so doing, to conquer the world. This command is more important today than it was then. It shows that children matter to God and should matter to us. As long as this world lasts, God wants children to be born. He needs each one of them for his coming kingdom. Young families should take heart in one of God's most beautiful commandments.

Bringing a child into the world today is more daunting than ever, and raising a child has never been more difficult. But it is well worth the challenge, and our future depends on it. As the well-known Hasidic saying goes, "If you save one child, you save the world."

We live in a time where there is not just fear but even hostility toward families and children. And though governments and policy-makers worry that the world is becoming overpopulated, children are still part of God's plan.

When the British commentator Malcolm Muggeridge asked Mother Teresa if she thought there were too many children in India – where many die of disease, starvation, and neglect – she gave him this remarkable answer: "I don't agree, because God always provides. He provides for the flowers and the birds, for everything in the world that he has created. And those little children are his life. There can never be enough!"

Founding new families and bringing children into the world will always be a step of faith. But it can give purpose to our lives and will be rewarding beyond all other ventures.

Johann Christoph Arnold
May 2012

1

The Childlike Spirit

Unless you change and become like little children,
you will never enter the kingdom of heaven.

Matthew 18:3

The Childlike Spirit

"CHILDREN WERE BROUGHT TO HIM so that he could lay his hands on them and pray. The disciples rebuked the people, but Jesus said, 'Let the children come to me, and do not hinder them; for the kingdom of heaven belongs to them'" (Matt. 19:13–14).

With these words, Jesus tells us that children are important. And his assertion that the kingdom of God belongs to them is a message we need still today: in our time no less than his, children are often not wanted.

Adults often fail to grasp how near to God children already are. We forget that, as Jesus says, "their angels always have access to my Father" (Matt. 18:10). *Angel* means *messenger.* Guardian angels are spiritual messengers, spirits sent by God to protect and guide children. Unlike these angels, and unlike children, we cannot see God. Yet we can see children, and we can receive them into our hearts. In receiving them, we receive Jesus himself (Luke 9:48).

How do we bring children to Jesus? First of all, we must believe in him ourselves, and come to him with trust and faith. In the New Testament we read how Simeon and Anna – two very old people – waited their whole lives for the Messiah, the "consolation of Israel." When Jesus was born, they welcomed the new baby with joy and belief. Now they could face death without fear and could live in peace (Luke 2:25–38).

As a pastor I am often asked to bless newborn babies, and it is one of the most wonderful things I do. Jesus himself says that "whoever welcomes one of these little children in my name welcomes me; and whoever welcomes me does not welcome me but the one who sent me" (Mark 9:37). This attitude of love and faith is what the childlike spirit is all about.

Everyone loves a new baby, but even babies can quickly test our patience and may soon seem to be a burden or inconvenience. But no matter how much trouble they bring, children are gifts from God. When we welcome them in this way, God will surely bless us and give us the strength to raise them. This should be an encouragement to all young families and to those who are thinking of founding a family. Especially when we face adversity, God is waiting to help us, providing we pray and ask, seek and knock (Matt. 7:7–11). Then doors will be opened.

In a time when childlike faith is despised and mocked like never before, we would do well to remember Jesus' words about becoming like children – and his promise that they will be the greatest in the age to come: "Unless you change and become like little children, you will never enter the kingdom of heaven. Therefore, whoever humbles himself like this child is the greatest in the kingdom of heaven" (Matt. 18:3–4).

For the sake of children everywhere, one wishes that this kingdom might come very soon.

2

Founding a Family

*For this reason a man will leave his father
and mother and be united to his wife,
and the two will become one flesh.*

Ephesians 5:31

Founding a Family

It is obvious on all fronts that the traditional nuclear family is on the way out. The family as we have known it for centuries has fallen apart, and children are increasingly being raised by grandparents or siblings. Rising divorce rates and growing pressures in the workplace mean that parents are passing on child care responsibilities to relatives.

Assisted reproductive technologies such as artificial insemination can have tragic consequences. Many children do not even know who their real parents are, or how they are related to other children. We seem to have forgotten that the health of society is dependent on the health of its families.

Fathers and mothers should always be the main role models in a child's life. All children long to know the two people who brought them into the world – to love them, and to be loved by them. Sadly, in too many cases, these two people are absent. Thankfully there are still people who believe that the traditional definition of a family is not only workable, but vital for survival. But this can only happen if we return to the simple teachings of Jesus, who taught us to love God and our neighbor as ourselves.

Jesus tells us to judge a tree by its fruit. A good tree cannot bear bad fruit, and a bad tree cannot bear good fruit. In the same way, a sound marriage can bless thousands of people, whereas a rotten one leaves a trail of devastation behind it.

For a marriage to endure, God must lead a man and woman to each other, and they must want him to hold them together. They must also desire his order, the husband serving his wife as spiritual head, and the wife serving her husband in return. Despite what many people think, such a relationship need not be restrictive or limiting; on the contrary, it is liberating. But it is possible only if Christ himself leads both partners.

If a husband is to lead his wife to God, he must respect and love her and not rule over her in a domineering way. He must allow himself to be guided by the Holy Spirit and remember that true leadership means service. The apostle Peter warns us that unless we consider and honor our wives, our prayers may be hindered (1 Pet. 3:7). Likewise, a woman should love and respect her husband.

Prayer is crucial in keeping a marriage healthy: "the family that prays together, stays together." Husband and wife should pray together daily – for their children, for each other, and for those around them. Given the hectic pace of life today, it may be helpful to set aside regular times for prayer: every morning before breakfast, for instance, and every night before going to sleep. Of course one can pray at other times, too, wherever one happens to be. But being busy or tired is not an excuse. How many of us spend time reading the paper, texting with friends, or watching TV every evening – but have no time for our spouses or for God?

Sociological studies have shown again and again that the two-parent family is the very best soil in which to raise children. Yet the world is full of single parents who must also be commended and encouraged. I have worked with many of them over the years, and have come to love them and their children in a special way. These children have as much to contribute to the world as anyone else – regardless of their family makeup or the circumstances of their birth and upbringing.

Still, marriage between one man and one woman, with the commitment of lifelong faithfulness, is the best foundation for a child's emotional health and stability. Broken family relationships, whether due to infidelity, divorce, or addiction, are devastating for a child and can leave emotional scars that last a lifetime.

Many people pray for God's will but follow it only when it matches their own. If we really love God we will seek to follow him whatever the outcome; we will sense that our deepest joy and greatest security lie in being faithful to him at all costs. By turning to God when our marriages falter, we will find the wisdom and strength with which to set things straight. He is the only sure foundation on which to build a family and raise children.

3

The Unborn Child

My frame was not hidden from you
when I was made in the secret place. When I was
woven together in the depths of the earth, your eyes
saw my unformed body.

───────────

Psalm 139:15–16

The Unborn Child

THE NINE MONTHS OF WAITING for a baby can deepen a couple's relationship and bring them closer to each other than any other time in their marriage. Especially for a young couple looking forward to their first child, there is a sense of excitement and the thrill of the unknown – a strange mixture of anxiety and joy. There is also awe before the mystery of new life and the responsibility of parenthood.

Few couples experience this sense of awe and mystery today. Pregnancy is seen less as a joyful affirmation of life than as a routine medical condition, and any secrets a mother might once have had are now trumpeted to friends and relatives alike in the form of test results and ultrasound scans. But is the development of a baby in its mother's womb only a biological process?

In his book *Innerland,* my grandfather Eberhard Arnold described the unborn child as a soul – a "little being waiting to be called out of eternity." If this is true, then pregnancy requires not only medical care but also reverence – and we should pay as much attention to a mother's spiritual needs as we do to her check-up appointments.

For the unborn as well as the living child, a secure and loving family life is of utmost importance. Even while still in the womb, a child can suffer if it does not feel nurturing love and tenderness. Thus bickering and fighting between husband and wife can harm the developing baby, just as do drinking or smoking. Of course, positive emotions and experiences will affect a baby to the same degree, so expecting parents should be encouraged to sing and pray together with their new child – even before it is born.

That an unborn child can share in the emotions of its mother is illustrated beautifully in the Gospel of Luke (Luke 1:41–44):

> When Elizabeth heard Mary's greeting, the child leaped in her womb. And Elizabeth was filled with the Holy Spirit and exclaimed with a loud cry, "Blessed are you among women, and blessed is the fruit of your womb. And why has this happened to me, that the mother of

my Lord comes to me? For as soon as I heard the sound of your greeting, the child in my womb leaped for joy."

In a similar way, the German writer Joseph Lucas says that a mother's thoughts are passed on to her child while it is still in the womb. Everything good in her – her love, her purity, and her strength – is planted into the child's being before it is born. In a certain way, he says, a mother's life during pregnancy lays the foundation for all later education. What comes after birth is "the unfurling and developing of what has already germinated in the soul."

When a mother finds out that she is pregnant, she should thank God. When Eve gave birth to Cain she said, "With the help of the Lord, I have brought a man into being" (Gen. 4:1). She did not say, "with the help of Adam," but "with the help of the Lord." God has a plan for each child, and we must stand in awe of it.

What about pregnancies that end in miscarriage? Doctors are quick to reassure couples that such a loss is nature's way of ending a life that was not to be, and in one way, this is true. Still, even the shortest pregnancy represents a life – a being with a soul. For this reason a couple should not be rushed over their loss, or be made to feel guilty about their grief. On the other hand, they must eventually find peace over the matter and accept God's will.

Of course, medical tests – like ultrasound exams – can give doctors useful information about a pregnancy, which can then guide decisions about labor and delivery. But such information is not always a blessing. In almost all cases nowadays, tests which reveal potential abnormalities and defects lead to a "termination."

Only God knows exactly how many innocent unborn children are aborted each year, but we know that this number reaches the millions. And abortion is murder, without exception. It destroys life and mocks God, in whose image every unborn baby is created. Therefore a woman who has had or is contemplating an abortion will always suffer torment of conscience. She can find healing only in Christ, who forgives every repentant heart.

Even the most persuasive arguments about quality of life or a mother's health should not sway us – nor should the case of rape. Who are we to decide whether or not a soul should reach the light of day? The most disabled child can give God glory. I have experienced this many times. And it is never we who have laid such a burden on the child's parents, but God – whose will works for the best in every situation (Rom. 8:28).

In a world obsessed with perfection and choice, we would do well to remember that God is a perfect creator, and that his children ought not to find fault, but simply praise:

> You created my inmost being; you knit me together in
> my mother's womb.
> I praise you because I am fearfully and wonderfully
> made;
> your works are wonderful, I know that full well.
> My frame was not hidden from you when I was made
> in the secret place.
> When I was woven together in the depths of the earth,
> your eyes saw my unformed body.
> All the days ordained for me were written in your book
> before one of them came to be.
>
> (Ps. 139:13–16)

4

Birth

A woman giving birth to a child has pain
because her time has come; but when her baby is born
she forgets the anguish because of her joy
that a child is born into the world.

John 16:21

Birth

Eᴠᴇʀʏ ᴛɪᴍᴇ ᴀ ʙᴀʙʏ ɪs ʙᴏʀɴ, eternity comes down
to our world. We feel joy in the arrival of a new human
being and know that in receiving an innocent soul, we
have received something from the hand of the Creator
himself. This is a life of unknown length in which, as the
poet Philip Britts writes, "a new note will be sounded,
and a new color revealed."

No matter how difficult the circumstances of a birth,
a baby's trusting gaze reminds us of God's love and
tenderness. It is as if he or she is surrounded by the pure
air of heaven. We can only marvel at the miracle of birth,
and at the fact that a unique and original new life has
been given by God.

Our modern way of looking at things can quickly
destroy this sense of wonder. For example, many
people see birth as a merely biological process, and
the new baby as a "product" of conception. But we are
reminded of God's role in the mystery of new life every

time a childless couple – after being told that they are infertile – leave their longing in God's hands and are then surprised by an unexpected pregnancy.

Dorothy Day writes that "even the most hardened, the most irreverent, is awed by the stupendous fact of creation. No matter how cynically or casually the world may treat the birth of a child, it remains spiritually and physically a tremendous event."

This attitude of awe and reverence should stay with us as we raise our children. Ultimately, our children do not belong to us – they are gifts entrusted to us by God. And if we hold on to this truth, we will want to bring them up in his stead.

I had seen many babies before I was married, but to experience my own first child was something quite different. Nothing could have prepared me for the moment when I realized, all of a sudden, that this was *our* baby and that it belonged to no one else. The responsibility of raising a child was now on our shoulders.

After a birth, the mother should receive special congratulations. It is simply a fact that she is the one who has done all the hard work – the one who has carried the baby for long months and endured the agony and anxieties of labor. Too often, we fathers do not appreciate what our wives have done.

A mother's life is in danger every time she gives birth. In my parents' time it was commonly said that a woman in labor had a foot in the grave, and this remains true today – despite the modern interventions which have made childbirth so much safer.

Therefore, if a birth goes well, a special prayer should be offered to God. After our own first child arrived, my wife and I lit a candle and thanked God for his protection – right in the hospital, along with the nurses and the doctors who had helped us.

5

Motherhood

Her children arise and call her blessed;
her husband also, and he praises her: "Many women
do noble things, but you surpass them all."

Proverbs 31:28–29

Motherhood

A TRUE MOTHER thinks day and night about the well-being of her children. She is the first to praise and comfort them and is also the first to protect them when she senses danger. It is she who has carried them and borne the pains of pregnancy and childbirth, and it is she who now continues to carry them in her heart. Her intuition is often clearer than her husband's, and she will not let him make light of her concerns or reassure her too easily. She will also be the first to turn to God on a child's behalf. Perhaps that is what inspired the old Jewish saying, "God could not be everywhere at once, so he gave each child a mother."

When a child cries at night, it is usually the mother who comes to its bedside first. She feels her child's pain instinctively and will bear it not only as a burden, but also as a privilege and a joy.

A mother's sensitivity and love are boundless. She will continue to hope for her children long after others have given up on them and pray for them even when everyone else has condemned them. Moreover, she will believe for them when they have ceased to believe.

A good mother is a role model for her immediate family and for everyone else she meets. Her joy makes those around her happy. And every woman is called to be a mother, whether married or single, and whether or not she has had children. People notice a woman who loves God and whose primary concern is serving others.

I cannot thank God enough for the love of my own mother, and for her deep relationship with my father. Even though they could never be called "religious" people, it was obvious to us seven children that our parents loved God, each other, and each one of us. And while it was clear that our father was head of the family, he never tolerated the slightest disrespect from us towards our mother.

Many women today resent the idea of motherhood, but they forget that it is a privilege as well as a task. Once regarded as the highest calling of woman, it is now pushed aside by "real" careers and viewed as an inconvenience or even an embarrassment. While this rebellion might be understandable in the case of oppression and abuse, it achieves nothing. How different family life could be if we admitted our confusion over the roles of man and woman; if we sought to rediscover God's plan for both, and regarded one another with respect and love!

Women today hold important jobs right up to the time they go into labor, and that is admirable. But when pregnancy and children require it, a woman's first priority should always be motherhood. She should be a mother first and foremost – and only after that, a doctor, teacher, lawyer, manager, or accountant. Far from regretting or resenting it, she ought to feel that motherhood is a gift, and that in God's eyes, there is no sacrifice more worthy than one made for a child.

One of my favorite examples of motherhood is found in the Old Testament. Hannah was barren for years but vowed that if she had a son, she would give him back to God. Her wish was finally granted, and even though she must have found it very hard, she kept her promise – she gave Samuel to the priest Eli to raise as a servant of God. Her childlike faith was rewarded not only once, but several more times: in time, she and her husband Elkanah were given five more children.

6

Fatherhood

Sons are a heritage from the Lord;
children a reward from him. Like arrows in the
hands of a warrior are sons born in one's youth.
Blessed is the man whose quiver is full of them.

Psalm 127:3–5

Fatherhood

GOD IS THE ULTIMATE EXAMPLE of fatherhood. He is the father of us all – young and old – and we are his children. There are no exceptions. Jesus says, "Call no one your father on earth, for you have one Father – the one in heaven" (Matt. 23:9). And even though he wants to be our father, he will never force himself on us. Instead, he wants us to feel our need for him and turn to him for help. This is why the Lord's Prayer begins with the important words, "Our Father."

God is waiting for us and will help us with any and every need. As Jesus says, "Is there anyone among you who, if your child asks for a fish, will give a snake instead? Or if the child asks for an egg, will give a scorpion? If you then, who are evil, know how to give good gifts to your children, how much more will the heavenly Father give the Holy Spirit to those who ask him" (Luke 11:11–13)!

This image of God as a loving role model cannot be emphasized enough. All children long for security – both emotional and physical. But a man who lacks character or is unsure of himself cannot provide his children with either. And when children are insecure, the consequences can be tragic.

How can men best give this assurance to their children? Anyone who plans to be a father and bring children into the world should first know that his children will be strongly affected by his own relationship with God. Those who build on this relationship will be blessed, whereas those who start a family without it will quickly founder. It is God who gives us fatherhood, and we are charged with leading our wives and children in his stead. This is why, in previous centuries, fathers were seen as irreplaceable. They may not have been the primary caregivers for their children, but they still bore the ultimate responsibility for the well-being of their families.

In the last one hundred years this has changed dramatically. In a century marked by war, unrest, and instability, more children than ever have grown up without a father in the house. Now people question the need for fathers at all: Who needs a father anyway? Why not a single mother? Or for that matter, two mothers? But such disregard for God's order is bound to have devastating consequences – not only for our children, but for the whole world.

Of course, true fatherhood entails far more than being physically present in the life of a child. There are plenty of men who remain emotionally distant from their children even though they live in the same house with them. And how many fathers confuse their children's hunger for love and attention with the desire for material things? All too often, such men try to buy their children's affection with gifts, when what their children really want is attention – a hug, a smile, or a bedtime story.

In the first five years of my life, my father's work kept him away from home for a total of three years. Although I know that this had certain negative effects on my early childhood, I never doubted my father's love. We were separated physically, but he remained a positive presence in my life, and my sisters and I never questioned his faithfulness to our mother or us. Neither did we use his absence as an excuse for misbehavior. Instead, the things he had instilled in us kept us going and spurred us on in supporting our mother.

This experience taught me that it is quality, and not quantity, that a child remembers. But this should not be construed as a selfish excuse. It is still important for fathers to spend time with their sons and daughters whenever they can. Often it is during the seemingly pointless times – those long hours in a car, for example – when an attentive father can be surprised by how his child opens up and tells him the most amazing things.

Of course, fatherhood begins even before the birth of a child. A husband should carry the burdens of his pregnant wife by showing love and understanding – and not frustration – when she is nauseated, tired, or tearful. If she needs bed rest he should be ready to take on still more, helping around the house and caring for any children already there. And he must be a source of cheerful encouragement and reassurance, and pray with her when she is overcome by fear or anxiety.

Sometimes a pregnancy will end in a miscarriage or stillbirth, and then a husband must be especially patient and understanding. Whereas the father may feel able to move on fairly quickly, the mother will feel this loss as the loss of an actual child. Even if she accepts this as part of God's plan, her grief must be acknowledged and in no way minimized.

Jesus – the only true man – was not afraid to see himself as a hen gathering its chicks. As fathers, we should not be ashamed to apply this same compassionate image to ourselves.

7

Creating a Home

*Whoever welcomes a little child
in my name welcomes me.*

Matthew 18:5

Creating a Home

IT IS ONE THING TO HAVE CHILDREN. To create a true home is quite another matter. Preparing a place of love and security for children is one of the most wonderful things parents can do. Such a home will reflect our love to God and our love for our children. Jesus tells us that whoever welcomes a child in his name welcomes him (Matt. 18:5).

Unfortunately, many parents lack a sense of what this means. Some simply have no time for their children: they are too busy to be bothered by them. Others remain emotionally absent from them even while they are physically present. You can see these parents in playgrounds and parks all over America and Europe, talking and texting on their phones while their children run around them. They may be physically present but their minds are elsewhere, planning for the next day or hour, and catching up on friends, news, and work.

A true home is created only when parents are ready to drop everything with joy, giving their hearts and minds to the children in front of them. Those who do this begrudgingly will reap bitter fruit. A child's emotional development depends on the love and attention he receives from his parents; those who do not receive these things at home will falter in the wider world which they must inevitably enter. What they need in the way of guidance, security, and love must be given now. Tomorrow is too late.

Parents who love their children will spend time with them as regularly as possible – and be there *for* them. Indoor activities like reading aloud, working on hobbies, and above all eating together give vital opportunities for interaction and a sense of togetherness. So do outdoor activities like playing ball, hiking, fishing, or back-packing. These provide the sort of positive experiences that children will not forget as they grow up, marry, and raise families of their own.

But being with our children – and being there for them – should not be confused with giving them things. How many of us come home from a business trip laden with gifts for our children, but still have no time to simply sit with them, to hear about what has been going on in their lives? How many children set these gifts aside, unsettled and still looking for real love? Even young children and infants can be negatively affected by having too many toys. By filling their beds and rooms with stuffed animals and books, we hinder the development of both personality and character – and we hinder appreciation, too.

Birthdays, graduations, and other celebratory occasions are an important part of home life. Aside from simply being happy times, these events can nurture and help children grow; they are times when we can thank God for them and let them know how much we love and appreciate them. But it is the priorities we set in our everyday lives that have the greatest impact on our children. The most extravagant party can never replace the security a child feels from time and attention given on a regular, daily basis.

Physical safety is no less important than emotional security. Parents who love their children will keep them away from hot stoves and open water, from high windows, moving vehicles, and poisonous medications. And while it is often said that modern parents err on the side of over-protection, this can never be used as an excuse for neglecting the proper supervision of young children.

Sometimes, creating a space for "family time" will require determination and energy, especially when children are playing outdoors with their friends, and you call them in for dinner. Most children will not be happy about such an interruption, but once a routine has been established, they will look forward to it.

Among my best childhood memories are the evenings when our family would sit on the stoop and listen to our father tell us stories about Jesus, about the early Christian martyrs and other men and women of faith throughout history. We lived in the backwoods of Paraguay, in South America, where there was no electricity. When darkness came, abrupt and early as it does in the subtropics, we lit candles and continued to sit in the flickering light. Our house was not far from the edge of a rainforest, and we often heard wild animals in the distance. When we were frightened we sang together, and our parents told us of the courage that comes from having a personal relationship with God. This became a reality for us.

But no matter how a family chooses to spend its time together, a few minutes at bedtime are always crucial. Younger children need the security of a good-night kiss, a reassuring word, and a short prayer before they go to sleep. Children who are afraid of the dark or of being alone – especially those who are unable to express their fears – should be reminded that they have guardian angels watching over them.

However, true security depends on more than comforting words. Children find their deepest emotional and inner security when their parents' love is demonstrated in deeds – and not just at bedtime, but from day to day. Speaking of family life in general, Mother Teresa says:

> We must not think that our love has to be extraordinary. But we do need to love without getting tired. How does a lamp burn? Through the continuous input of small drops of oil. These drops are the small things of daily life: faithfulness, small words of kindness, a thought for others, our way of being quiet, of looking, of speaking, and of acting. They are the true drops of love that keep our lives and relationships burning like a lively flame.

8

The Role of Grandparents

Grandchildren are the crown of the aged.

Proverbs 17:6

The Role of Grandparents

GRANDPARENTS are the most wonderful thing in the world – at least many children think so. But many of us are ambivalent about their role in family life. Some families are blinded by the notion that in-laws cannot get along together, and by accepting this stereotype as fact, they harm what could otherwise be a meaningful relationship. But doesn't God want us all to live in peace? After all, he meant husband and wife to be one, and naturally each of them has parents.

Unfortunately, many grandparents today languish in nursing homes or retirement communities while their children and grandchildren live far away. This may be a reflection of the economic and social realities of our time, but it is still not a good thing. In previous centuries, it was unthinkable for children to abandon their parents and grandparents. The word "family" meant "extended family" without exception. And this extended family can be a tremendous blessing.

Those of us lucky enough to live close to our grandchildren need not be convinced of this truth. Our children's care for us reflects their gratitude for the years we spent caring for them. In turn, we share our joy in them and their children by playing cards, hunting and fishing, and even teaching them to drive. Hopefully we also serve as role models for them.

My wife and I thank God that we are grandparents, and we look forward to becoming great-grandparents within the next few years. Yet it is clear to us that no matter how much we love our grandchildren, we must let our children find their own way in bringing them up. This can be hard, especially when their ideas about education differ from ours. But we cannot take away the primary responsibility they have for their own children, which will remain with them long after we are gone.

All the same, young couples should be encouraged to turn to their parents for advice. Why shouldn't grandparents pass on their wisdom, even if much of it was gained through mistakes? And those who live far away should not use distance as an excuse. They can remain actively involved in their children's and grandchildren's lives by writing letters and calling on the phone – if not exploiting the marvels of modern technology to a good purpose. More often than not, their help and care will be welcomed and not resented.

Grandparents should feel free to advise, but should never interfere. Obviously there are exceptions. In matters of safety or negligence, a grandparent has no choice other than to intervene. But the best help may be to support parents in practical ways: when a grandchild is sick, for example, or when parents have been taxed to their limits for any other reason.

Every grandchild delights in special attention – a story, a cookie, extra help with homework, or a walk outdoors. Of course, grandparents who live far away from their grandchildren will have to find other ways to show love: a postcard or gift, a phone call, or a special visit. But they can always pray for their grandchildren, especially as they reach the difficult teenage years.

Regardless of a child's age, the times spent with a grandparent will always be enriching. Such moments will be experienced as oases of comfort and quiet for the child, and the grandparent will see them as opportunities for love. In the end, both will be blessed.

9

The First Years

Train a child in the way he should go, and when he is old he will not turn from it.

Proverbs 22:6

The First Years

Educators have long held that the first five years of a child's life are the most formative; whatever children experience in this period will influence them for the rest of their lives. The nineteenth-century German educational reformer Froebel writes that a person's spiritual life is formed to a great degree by the experiences of early childhood. A child's future relationship to parents, to God, to society at large, and even to nature depends chiefly on his or her development during this period.

Recent studies have confirmed this scientifically. In light of this fact and the tremendous responsibility it places on every parent, it is vital that the bonds between father, mother, and baby are nurtured beginning at birth. Parents should remember that God has given the child to them, and that it is their responsibility to steer the child on the path that fulfills God's purpose for him or her.

The significance of interacting with a baby cannot be emphasized enough. My mother always said that education starts in the cradle. Babies should be held, stroked, and caressed. They should be sung to, talked to, and smiled at. Most important, they should be loved unconditionally.

But parents must guard against seeing their children through rose-colored glasses. I have seen the lives of young people destroyed because when they were small, their parents could not say "no" to them: they saw their children only as "cute" and failed to discipline them. These parents were held hostage by their own children, who then grew up spoiled, unable to accept disappointment or hardship, and unwilling to take responsibility for their actions.

As children become toddlers, they should be stimulated and encouraged with simple games, rhymes, and songs. Their mental potential at this stage is unrivaled, and what they do not take in now will be absorbed only with great difficulty later. That is why experts speak of a "window of opportunity" that will never be opened as widely again.

To be sure, development cannot be measured only in terms of learning or achievement. Children's emotional and spiritual development is equally important, and this is often acquired when they are by themselves. Time spent alone is crucial for the development of the imagination and will teach children to entertain themselves without adult involvement. Hours spent in daydreams and quiet play instill a sense of security and provide a necessary lull in the rhythm of the day. All too often, however, adults needlessly disturb and pester children with their intrusions. They cannot pass a baby without picking it up, holding, kissing, or doing something to it. If the child resists or struggles, they feel hurt, and what was a happy scene only moments before is now one of anger and frustration. Froebel takes this idea a step further and maintains that uninterrupted play is a prerequisite for uninterrupted work. The child who plays thoroughly will become a thorough, determined adult.

At every point of contact, loving consideration for the inner disposition of the child – for the spirit of simplicity, honesty, and vulnerability – is crucial. Raising children does not mean molding them according to our own wishes and ideas. It means helping them to become what they already are in God's mind.

"Unlearning" our adult mindsets is never easy. Even the disciples were indignant when children pushed through them to get closer to Jesus. When there are children around, things don't go as planned. Furniture gets scratched, flower beds trampled, new clothes torn, and toys lost or broken. Children want to handle things and play with them. They want to have fun, and they need space to be rambunctious and noisy.

Thus for the parents of small children, the first years can seem overwhelmingly strenuous at times – and at the end of a long day, children can even seem to be more of a bother than a gift. They are not porcelain dolls but rascals with sticky fingers and runny noses. They cry at night. Yet if we have children, we must welcome them as they are.

10

Teaching Respect

*Honor your father and your mother,
so that you may live long in the land
the Lord your God is giving you.*

Exodus 20:12

Teaching Respect

ALL OF US ARE familiar with the biblical commandment that is the cornerstone of child rearing: Honor
father and mother. But what does it mean? On one
level, of course, it simply means that children must learn
respect. In the eyes of small children, father and mother
stand for God; if they do not honor their parents, how
can they ever learn to honor him? On another level, it
places a burden on every parent: the responsibility of
seeing that this commandment is obeyed.

Honor starts with respect for authority, with the
"fear of God" and the similar "fear" of parents, who
stand in God's stead. Obviously this does not mean
that children should be afraid of God or their parents.
Rather, it means that as they grow up they must learn
to overcome their inborn self-centeredness, and yield
to others when the situation calls for it.

But if respect is achieved by authoritarian means,
it will eventually breed anger and rebellion. Instead,

children must find a willingness to submit to authority that is born of love and reverence. This takes effort. It can be gained only gradually, and must be fostered in an atmosphere of love and trust.

Yet because respect is a basic part of every wholesome relationship, it is vital that it be taught starting at a very early age. In my experience, it must be established within the first four years. In most families with young children this task will fall to the mother, since she is the one most likely to be at home with her children during the working day. Of course a husband should always support his wife, but it is imperative that she establish an authority of her own, too; otherwise, her children will not obey her when she is alone.

At times this is easy: guiding a child with a gentle word or appealing to its inborn love. Just as frequently, however, it will demand a struggle. Then the most important thing is that the struggle is fought through and won. Disrespect may seem manageable in small children – you can always use a "time out" until they are ready to listen – but costs a painful contest of wills in teenagers. All the same, if a battle seems inevitable, it should be met head on and fought to the end.

Still, respect must be earned and not only demanded. When children lack respect for adults, it is usually because the adults in their lives lack respect for them. Even if you feel you deserve a child's respect, digging in your heels for the sole sake of asserting authority will backfire. Your long-term relationship with the child will suffer, and you will achieve nothing other than a hardened heart.

My father felt strongly that a parent's authority must be grounded in love: "If we as parents love God with all our heart and soul, our children will have the right reverence for us, and we will have reverence for our children and for the wonderful mystery of becoming and being a child. Reverence for the spirit which moves between parent and child is the basic element of true family life."

Jesus says that there is no greater love than to lay down one's life for a friend (John 15:13). A father should lead his family with such love and respect, and must be ready to die for his wife and children. This conviction will inspire his children to honor both him and their mother.

Everything in a child's life hinges on respect for father and mother. Such an attitude will engender respect both for self and for others, which in turn will lead a child to the service of God and humankind.

11

Spoiling Your Child

The rod of correction imparts wisdom,
but a child left to himself disgraces his mother.

Proverbs 29:15

Spoiling Your Child

Despite the fact that millions of children around the globe grow up in acute poverty, most children in our society have far more than they need. We are raising a whole generation of children who can only be called spoiled. We parents are often quick to blame the materialism of society at large, or the steady diet of commercials our children see daily, but in actual fact the problem begins long before our children are exposed to any of these forces. In my experience, pampered children are the product of pampered parents – parents who insist on always getting their own way, and whose lives are structured around the illusion that instant gratification brings happiness.

Children are spoiled not only by an overabundance of food, toys, and clothing, but by giving in to their whims. This is bad enough when they are still in the playpen, but as they grow older, the problem gets much worse. Children who feel relatively certain that they will get their way are bound to put up a good fight when their wishes are frustrated or denied, and their demands can quickly define their entire relationship with their parents. How many harried parents spend all of their energy simply trying to keep up with their children's demands? And how many more give in to their children just to keep them quiet?

Children are also pampered when they are given too many choices. Of course children need to learn to make decisions, but those who constantly offer them an array of choices – whether between foods, flavors, drinks, or activities – do them a grave disservice. Children who face three different brands of cereal at the breakfast table are no happier than those whose food is set before them. Too much choice breeds indecision, finicky eating behaviors, and ungratefulness. In fact, children crave limits. When their boundaries are clearly defined, they thrive.

It is also possible to spoil children by over-stimulating them. Though children should be exposed to a variety of activities wide enough to keep their attention and to encourage their imagination, we do them a disservice if we feel obliged to offer them a constant diet of new thrills and experiences. They must learn that in real life, there are many things they simply cannot do or have.

If given too much rein, children will become little tyrants at home and at school, and as they grow older, they will go to any length to get what they want. All too soon they will be impulsive, demanding teenagers, and what was once plain discontent is now unmanageable rebellion.

How, then, can we raise our children without pampering them? From the Book of Proverbs to the journals of modern medicine, the wisdom is the same: discipline your child. Set boundaries, say "no" as often or more often than you say "yes," and do not feel sorry for your children when they throw a tantrum and turn away with sullen disappointment. Even if the going is at first tough, well-disciplined children will end up as appreciative, considerate, and self-assured adults – whereas those who get their way will be insecure, selfish, and dishonest.

Paul compares God to an earthly parent, and writes that God disciplines and chastises those whom he loves (Heb. 12:6). If we really desire to love our children as God loves us, we will do the same.

12

Discipline

Listen to your father's instruction and do not forsake your mother's teaching. They will be a garland to grace your head and a chain to adorn your neck.

Proverbs 1:8–9

Discipline

IN AN AGE WHEN DISCIPLINE of any kind is regarded as abuse, it is tempting to dismiss the Old Testament proverbs about sparing the rod and spoiling the child. All the same, we can find wisdom in the ones that speak about discipline in a general sense, even if we reject physical punishment, as I do.

When children are conscious of having done something wrong without a consequence, they learn a bad lesson. Especially when they are young the misdeed itself may be quite small, but if not confronted, it will lead to far worse behavior in the future. The six-year-old who is not disciplined for taking a handful of coins from his parents' dresser may well be shoplifting at sixteen.

But discipline means more than just catching children in the act, and it does not mean suppressing their will in favor of our own. It means guiding them to choose right over wrong. It means teaching self-denial as a valuable character trait, not an old-fashioned deprivation.

Effective discipline starts at a very early age. Already in the first few months, babies find out that their crying summons attention and concern. But a mother who responds to every whimper has already lost the battle. All babies need to be soothed, but they need not be picked up every time they cry. If they do not learn to deny themselves in the very first years, when will they?

To hold out firmly and consistently against a child's will is often irksome. Yet parents who prize comfort above the effort of discipline will find that in the long run, their children will only become more and more troublesome. All children resist at the beginning, but they will eventually thrive on routine.

How should a child be disciplined? Scolding and nagging frequently, especially for minor indiscretions, often escalates to impatience and anger, and then both parent and child will end up in a shouting match. In the same way, parents who explain and defend every action they take will end up exhausted and unsure of themselves.

Rather, parents should choose actions over words. One of the simplest forms of discipline is "time out" – putting a child who has misbehaved in another room for a few minutes. A child punished in this way will soon feel bored or lonely and want to return to play; when he or she is quiet, the episode should be forgiven and the child allowed to move on.

Corporal punishment, however, has no place. My grandfather, an educator, called it a "declaration of moral bankruptcy" and felt that it was not only harmful but futile. This is because even the strongest discipline will be ineffective unless accompanied by love. Without warmth and kindness, and without respect, any form of discipline will sooner or later lead to rebellion.

Thus good discipline depends on trust between parent and child. Thankfully my siblings and I had such a relationship with our parents. When I was eight years old, I upset my father so much that he felt he needed to punish me severely. As he was about to spank me, I looked up at him and said, "Papa, I'm sorry. Do what you need to do. I know you still love me." To my astonishment, he leaned down and hugged me and said, "Son, I forgive you." My words had completely disarmed him. The incident taught me a lesson I have never forgotten: Don't be afraid to discipline your children, but the moment you feel remorse on their part, be sure there is forgiveness on yours.

Consistency is also key. If you disagree with your spouse over how to handle an incident, don't discuss it in front of your children – or they will soon be playing you off against each other. And don't change your approach just because the living room is full of guests. Bite your lip and do what you need to do; either way, you will have to deal with your child after the guests have gone, and your long-term relationship to him is far more important than the impression you make on others.

Children cannot be expected to obey every command unquestioningly, and it may be necessary to explain some things to them. A child should usually have no choice but to obey. However, if direct conflict arises, it is imperative that you win. The main thing is that you set the limits and don't let your children set them for you. If you are able to enforce limits consistently and with love, they will sooner or later be able to set limits for themselves.

No matter how often you need to discipline your children, never humiliate them. Don't talk about their weaknesses or mistakes in front of other adults, and never compare them to other children. It is easy to label a child as "difficult," but it is never right or just. Like children, we must not only forgive the wrongs of the previous hour and day, but also forget them, and start every day anew. And we must believe in the positive goal of discipline, as Proverbs 19:18 so eloquently says: "Reprove your child, for in this there is hope."

13

Explaining Life, Death, and Suffering

For my thoughts are not your thoughts,
neither are your ways my ways.

———————

Isaiah 55:8

Explaining Life, Death, and Suffering

In speaking about birth, death, and the other mysteries of human existence with children, it is good to remember that all of life is in God's hands. Children understand this truth more easily than adults. Their minds are simple and their questions straightforward; if our answers go beyond what they have asked, we only confuse them.

All life comes from God and goes back to God, and if we really believe this, our fears about death – and our children's fears – should be allayed. The Bible tells us that God holds power even over death, and how wonderful it will be when Jesus comes back – how the trumpet will sound, and how we will all be made alive, even more than we are now (1 Cor. 15:52).

Telling children about birth need not be difficult. Most children will accept and understand new life quite simply, as a gift that comes from God, and we must take care not to burden them with more information than they have asked for. Of course, what they ask about will also change with age, and as they grow older, we cannot hide from them the facts of human reproduction. Even then, reverence for God as the source and giver of life will enable them to accept our answers, and to respect their own – and other's – bodies.

At a surprisingly young age, children may also wonder why God allows so much suffering in the world – why he allows poverty, war, and evil, and why it often seems that the devil is stronger than God. Such thoughts may never occur to some children, but can cause considerable worry to others.

When children ask about these things, parents should remind them that despite sin, pain, and injustice, God is all-powerful, and that his love will rule in the end. Explain to them that all the pain of the world – especially the suffering of innocent people – is also a deep pain to God. Help them to see that it is not God's fault when people hate each other and start wars. And point them to the story of Adam and Eve, who questioned God's word and then disobeyed him by eating from the tree of knowledge. This is how sin came into the world; before the fall of man, everything and everyone lived in harmony and peace. That is how God wanted it to be, and that is how it will be again when his peaceable kingdom comes on the earth.

In this way children can be helped to understand that suffering and death are a part of God's plan. Naturally we should not frighten them, but it will not harm them to know that they will also suffer – and die – one day. In fact, this is something they can look forward to, providing we also pass on to them a living faith.

We can do this best by admitting our own fears to our children and praying with them, while at the same time emphasizing the peace we find when we trust in God. In this way, children will learn, by example, to cope with the suffering they are bound to face sooner or later.

We must also be vigilant in taking time for children who are dealing with insecurities. Maybe a friend or relative has been injured or even died, or a teacher has brought up a recent accident or natural disaster in class. Either way, what may seem a small incident to us can loom large in a child's mind. But listening to fears, answering questions, and pointing the child to God can bring peace.

Older children can also be reminded that even if they are afraid, there may be others worse off than they. This will teach them compassion. And we can reassure them that God will not burden us with more than we can bear.

14

Religious Education

The commandments that I give you today are to be upon your hearts. Impress them on your children.

Deuteronomy 6:6–7

Religious Education

RELIGIOUS EDUCATION is always a hot-button topic. Despite the legal right to profess one's faith, public schools generally reject God and embrace hedonism, disrespect, and irreverence. The values that were taken for granted just a generation ago are now questioned, and any references to God – to Jesus, to creation, and to faith – are increasingly forbidden.

In many quarters, marriage has been redefined, and the idea that a family should be headed by one man – with one woman at his side – is derided as old-fashioned and restrictive. Religious symbols and celebrations connected to Christmas and Easter are pushed aside, supposedly out of respect for non-believers, and "tolerance" has become a god.

All of this is like pulling out the rug on which our children stand. It has nothing to do with respect for other traditions and cultures. Instead, it is a concerted effort by a godless society to destroy the framework which once held Western civilization together.

Of course, it is foolishness to believe that we can make God disappear. Whatever we do, God will be there. God was there long before we existed and will be there long after we are gone. It is imperative, then, that we as parents boldly pass on to our children the religious values we hold dear, regardless of the consequences.

Our children crave a foundation to stand on. Their emotional stability as adults will depend on what we teach them when they are young. How, then, should we lead them to God? For one thing, we can never force our values down their throats. Instead, we must let them feel and know the impact of our own faith on a daily basis.

God's spirit does not let itself be tied down to the space of a lesson or a memorized text. Thus we cannot depend on pious words, but need actions and deeds with which to pass our faith on to our children.

What we teach now will continue to bear fruit for years to come. If our own children learn to honor father and mother and God, they will pass this commandment on. And if they learn to discern the difference between right and wrong, they will be equipped to teach the same discernment to their children.

We can bring God to children best by pointing them to nature. Jesus himself used parables and metaphors from the natural world to illustrate a point. Still today, children will sense God behind a brilliant sunset or a starry sky; they can imagine him in the roaring wind or in a violent storm. They will be the first to perceive that behind the beauty of the earth is a Creator, who also dwells in their hearts.

We can also teach children about God by reading stories to them: by telling them about the life of Jesus, and explaining to them the meaning behind Christmas and Easter. There is no better time than the weeks before Christmas for reading aloud the Old Testament prophecies concerning the Messiah, or for telling about the hosts of angels that announced Christ's birth. In the same way, children can be taught about Easter by hearing about Christ's suffering on the cross, followed by his joyful resurrection.

Memorizing short verses from Scripture can also be a way to teach faith. Children who learn important passages by heart will have a rock to stand on in later life and will find comfort and reassurance through God's word when hard times come. Music can point a person to God as well: my own children began hearing Handel's *Messiah* when they were quite small and say that their faith is strengthened by it still today.

Thanking and praising God is as important as asking him for help. Whether by saying grace before a meal or praying at bedtime, children should be taught to thank God for all they have – for parents and family, friends, food, and a roof over their heads. Reminding them that not all children have what they have opens their eyes to the needs of others.

In a time when polarizing rhetoric and hateful arguments rule the public square, it is crucial that our homes be oases of inner strength and security – that we as parents model the values by which we want our children to live. This is the greatest gift we can give our children, and the most important aspect of education.

15

When Children Suffer

Then I would still have this consolation –
my joy in unrelenting pain – that I had not denied
the words of the Holy One.

Job 6:10

When Children Suffer

WHEN A CHILD SUFFERS AND DIES, it is the mother who (apart from the child) feels the pain most deeply. I have experienced this personally in my life. Two of my sisters died in infancy, and though I never saw them alive, I know what need their sickness and death brought to both of my parents, especially to my mother.

My wife and I lost a granddaughter at the age of one month. She had Trisomy 13, and though she did not live long, she affected thousands of people and moves hearts still today. A poem written about her by one of my other granddaughters says it best:

> Though her little life was short,
>   the light did not die out –
> It melted all our hearts and now we can shout;
> Our hearts are opened wide to the message of the child:
> Jesus will come again, Amen.

Anyone who has been at the bedside of a dying child will know what I mean when I speak of the fight for life that goes on in each soul and body. This fight is independent of the parents' longing for the child to live; it is independent even of the child's own waiting and longing to be released from pain.

This tenacious will to live is in every person, not only in children. It is even present in the elderly. They may be on the threshold of eternity, completely ready to go, praying for God to free them from their misery. Yet when their time comes – even when the body has begun to shut down – it is still hard to let go of life.

God is with every child who suffers. Often this may seem too difficult, even impossible, to believe. Why should my child, why should we, have to bear the burden of pain? Why does God give us a child to love and then take it away from us again? How can our grief possibly serve any purpose?

Even though no one can answer such deep questions satisfactorily, we know that none of us is exempt from suffering. If we can accept this, even without under-standing it, we will find peace and meaning in it. At the very least we should be able to see that suffering can point us to God and to compassion for others.

More than adults, children often have a natural inclination to faith, because they are so close to God. When we experience such faith, we should be careful not to hinder it, but nurture it so that it may become a foundation on which future storms can be faced.

My father, Heinrich Arnold, who lost his first child to an incurable illness when she was only three months old, writes:

> Children are closer than anyone else to the heart of Jesus, and he points to them as an example for us. The fact that children have to suffer is very strange. It is as if they are bearing someone else's guilt, as if they are suffering because of the fall of creation. In a way they seem to be paying the wages of sin – even though it is sin in which they have taken no active part as yet.
>
> Perhaps the suffering of children has a close connection with the greatest suffering ever endured: God's suffering, Christ's suffering for lost creation. Therefore the suffering of a child always has deep significance.

In a world which aims to avoid suffering at all cost, we can never forget that it was through suffering that Christ redeemed the world. Seen in this way, suffering can change us and deepen our belief. Without faith, it can make us bitter, but with faith it can save us – even when it is hard to bear.

16

The Special Child

Has not my hand made all these things,
and so they came into being?

———

Isaiah 66:2

The Special Child

J ESUS SAYS that if anyone wants to follow him, he
must first deny himself and take up his cross (Mark
8:34). These words were addressed not only to the
people of his time, but also to us today. Each of us
who desires to follow Christ must be willing to carry the
burden laid on us by God.

Because the cross every person carries is different, we
tend to look at others and compare our lot with theirs.
We think how athletic – or handsome, articulate, or
gifted – the other person is, and we wonder whether they
have any cross to bear at all. Envy makes us dissatisfied.

Clearly, every man, woman, and child has a burden
to carry. Even the apostle Paul had a "thorn in his flesh."
He asked God to remove it, but God answered, "My
grace is sufficient for you, for my power is made perfect
in weakness" (2 Cor. 12:8). If we accept this grace, we
will be able to bear the heaviest load. Strange as this may
seem, it can even become a blessing.

Today, with the common availability of sophisticated prenatal tests, fetal abnormalities are often discovered early in pregnancy. Sometimes, this can lead to life-saving intrauterine surgery or therapy. But in many if not most other cases, doctors subsequently advise an abortion. They argue that this is in the best interest of both child and parents, and suggest that allowing such a child to be carried to term is not only unfair but irresponsible, because the child will place a burden on society.

Yet abortion is always wrong. God has a specific purpose in mind for every person – for every tiny being that is conceived. No matter how short its life, or how difficult, every new child bears a certain message from God. None of us can presume to know exactly what this message is. All the same, the message is there, if only we open our hearts to it.

My wife and I were reminded of this truth when one of our daughters gave birth to her fifth child in 2008. Stephanie was born with Trisomy 13 – a condition that cannot be cured – and her little face was disrupted by a cleft palate. She lived only a month, but we quickly grew to love her, and soon saw in her a beauty that was much deeper than physical perfection: the deep peace of God which she radiated to all those who surrounded her crib. When she died, we wept and wept; though we had known she would not live, she had been an angel in our midst, and brought us a message of heaven that surpassed words.

Of course, the discovery that a newborn child is disabled can be deeply unsettling. Parents often blame themselves, or wonder what they might have done to deserve such a bad outcome. But as natural as such thoughts may seem, we should not give them room. Rather, we should try to see the situation from a deeper perspective – as a blessing which can lead us closer to each other and to God.

When Jesus and his disciples met a man who was blind from birth, his disciples asked him, "Rabbi, who sinned – this man or his parents, that he was born blind?" Jesus answered, "Neither he nor his parents sinned; he was born blind so that God's works might be revealed in him" (John 9:1–3). This was surely the case with Stephanie. Her abnormalities came to us from God, as a revelation of his mighty works. The challenge to us is whether or not we can accept such revelations, and whether or not we welcome them.

Many parents of disabled children do not see them as a gift. All too often they are impatient, even intolerant, or else overprotective. To them, a disabled child hurts the family pride. They regard the child as a disappointment and feel dishonored and ashamed. Neighbors, relatives, and friends often aggravate such a situation with insensitive remarks, as do those doctors and therapists who suggest that the child be moved into an institution.

How different things would be if we saw disabled children as gifts, and not burdens! When friends of ours gave birth to a child with Down syndrome in 1967, they rejoiced – as did we. Louisa had a serious cardiac defect but lived her twenty-nine years to the full. She radiated joy and excitement wherever she went, and touched the most sophisticated and guarded people with her forthright manner and infectious laughter. Even as she died, she told her friends and family, "I'm thinking about LIFE!"

Children like her are not wanted today. True, the prospect of a disabled child can seem more than a family is able to face. Even the strongest parents will need support at times, and they should never feel guilty when they seek or accept help. Those of us who do not have to cope with such a child should offer our practical support where we can, by taking the child into our home for a night or a weekend to let the parents relax and find new strength.

Given their special needs, it is easy to see why such children are often treated differently from others. All too often, parents give in to their every whim, and spoil them. Yet pampering such children is a great disservice, because it limits their entire future – their physical and mental development, and their emotional independence.

All children need the warmth of physical affection, and disabled children need it perhaps even more than others. But they should not be babied with constant hugs, kisses, and treats. Rather, they should be encouraged to use their abilities to the full, and treated as normally as possible. This is not to say that they should be pushed to perform, or take on responsibilities beyond their capabilities. All the same, it is amazing what firm expectations can do. As a pastor, I have seen time and again how an optimistic approach can help the most incapacitated child achieve mobility, independence, and self-worth.

It is tempting to wonder why one person is born with mental or physical disabilities, while the next is perfectly healthy. Yet we must trust that everything that happens in life, whether good or difficult, has a purpose. We must believe that God can turn any affliction into a blessing if we humbly accept whatever he sends. Christ comes to us in the form of a stranger, a beggar, and an angel. Why should he not also come in the form of a disabled child?

17

Adoption

*Religion that God our Father accepts
as pure and faultless is this: to look after
orphans and widows in their distress.*

James 1:27

Adoption

ASIDE FROM THE MILLIONS OF LIVES snuffed out by abortion every year, thousands more children are born unwanted. Some are rejected by parents who cannot face the demands of feeding yet another mouth; others are abandoned because they are malformed or crippled. And these infants are not only abandoned in hospitals and clinics. Increasing numbers have been left in garbage cans and dumpsters by teenagers who cannot cope with them, or by adults who are abusive, addicted to alcohol and drugs, or simply unable to make ends meet.

Obviously it is the biological parents of such children who bear the greatest obligation toward them. Yet at the same time, the abandonment of babies and small children is an indictment on all of us. As long as there are slums and ghettos – and exploitation and unemployment – those of us who enjoy economic security bear a guilt, too.

How can we help women who feel so overwhelmed that they refuse to care for a baby they themselves have carried? My grandfather – who was clearly opposed to abortion – stated that it was wrong to protest against it without giving women and families a practical alternative. In the same way, we cannot condemn people who abandon or give up their children unless we address the very real pressures that drive them to such a drastic decision. This will not be an easy task, but it is clear that churches, shelters, clinics, and social workers are not doing enough.

It can take years of waiting and thousands of dollars to adopt a child, and matching hopeful couples with unwanted children can be extremely difficult. In some cases this is because a child does not meet the high standards or particular wishes of its prospective parents; in other cases, government agencies have been forced to go to great lengths to protect clients from illegal operations. But it is clear that something radical needs to be done to make adoption easier and less economically burdensome, while remaining safely regulated.

Even when an adoption goes through, raising the adopted child is not easy. Many such children are victims of abuse and neglect, or the circumstances of their birth have left them scarred in soul and spirit. They may also have underlying medical or psychiatric problems.

Still, they must be welcomed with unconditional love. Already one hundred years ago, the German pastor Blumhardt offered this still-timely advice:

> Whoever adopts children must accept them with all their ingratitude, or it will not go well. To take in children and expect thanks from them is unnatural. Children never show special thanks to those who feed and clothe them, apart from showing love the way children do. They take it quite for granted that we won't let them go hungry or naked, and that we won't do just the minimum if we could do a little more. And they will feel they have a *right* to this, whoever cares for them.
>
> Many who adopt children, however, think that these children should acknowledge them – that they should feel awed by the fact that people who do not owe them anything have taken them in out of compassion. But that is just what they do *not* feel, so we should not demand it of them.
>
> Love them without expecting thanks, even if they cause you trouble; you have to accept them along with their naughtiness. They will feel this and will love you for it, but without words.

Often foster children are given what they need, but without love, and they are made to feel this even in words. It hurts them deeply and can even give rise to hatred in their hearts...

Foster children do not want to have fewer privileges than the children they live with; they have a sharp eye, and if they see differences, it hurts them terribly. Why is that? They are simply children, and they do not see why one child should have more than another.

If you adopt children, adopt them fully so they can be free to simply be children and can make any childlike demand of you.

We would do well to remember that Jesus said, "Whoever receives a child in my name, receives me" (Matt. 18:5). Surely this wonderful promise applies to adoptive parents – to every couple that welcomes a child into their home.

18

Children and Sin

*If we claim to be without sin, we deceive ourselves
and the truth is not in us. If we confess our sins, he is
faithful and just and will forgive us our sins and
purify us from all unrighteousness.*

1 John 1:8–9

Children and Sin

DESPITE THE SINFUL INCLINATION of every human being, children are closer to God than we are, and if anyone will enter the kingdom of heaven, it is they. But it is a mistake to regard children as naturally good – to see them through rose-colored glasses and to excuse everything they do as merely childish.

We must remember that when children do wrong, they do not always mean things the way we adults might. But it is still wrong to think that they are not susceptible to sin. They are, and must be helped to choose right over wrong again and again. Because their will is still completely free, they must not be allowed to fall prey to evil, but must be won over for the good.

Harshness and cruelty of any kind is always wrong, but so is permissiveness. Thus discipline and even punishment are still necessary, but this depends on a relationship of love and trust. If we love God and want to guide our children to him, we will find the biblical "salt" that true love demands.

Regardless of how young a child is, he can always learn to apologize after doing something wrong – and mean it. Humility takes a lifetime to learn, and parents who don't instill it in their children when they are small will discover that it gets harder as they grow older. Thus the saying, "Little children, little problems; big children, big problems" should not be dismissed as an old cliché; parents who conquer stubbornness in a three-year-old will be far ahead of those who wait to tackle the same problem in a teenager.

Sometimes bad behavior is a cry for attention or a reaction to a lack of love. In these cases we should not jump to conclusions or assume a child has consciously done wrong. Children are the center of their own little universes; they see the whole world around them from their perspective. When they take something to themselves enthusiastically, it is not because they are selfish, but because they have become absorbed in it. Such natural self-centeredness is not in itself wrong. All the same, children will need help to see beyond themselves as they grow older.

When children show off or hurt others – or when they lie or steal – it is tempting to blame only them. But wise parents will also look at themselves, and wonder what it is in them that might have led to such behavior. Blumhardt advises us to turn the sword against ourselves, and to cut out the sin in our own hearts – sin that may be resurfacing in our offspring.

Children who are jealous or quarrelsome should be helped to work out their differences in a positive manner. Children also have an amazing capacity for compassion, and our main focus should be to affirm this capacity, and not to fight their selfish inclinations. In this way, they will begin to grasp the meaning of the two greatest commandments: "Love God with all your heart, mind, and soul," and "Love your neighbor as yourself" (Matt. 22:37–39).

It is important, too, for them to learn that life is not a level playing field – that it is not "fair." Those who can accept this at an early age will be better equipped to handle the cruelties of adulthood. Still, we must not ignore the effects of a child's personality and place in a family or class. Is he or she the oldest child? The youngest? Don't show favoritism, and remember that generosity is taught best by example, not by lengthy lectures.

Often embarrassment or shame will cause children to wriggle out of something by telling a half-truth. If they are really afraid of the consequences for what they have done, they may tell an outright lie. This should not surprise us. Still, if a child has been dishonest, it is important to establish the facts, and then help the child face them and make amends.

If you think a child has lied but aren't certain, don't press him into making a confession. Trying to catch a child "in the act" or probing into all possible motives does great harm; it weakens self-confidence and destroys trust. Simply let the child know that you are unhappy about the situation and leave the door open for setting the matter straight later. Children almost always respond to such a suggestion, and may even wake their parents in the middle of the night to admit to a lie because their conscience bothers them. When the truth comes out, applaud them for having made a clean slate. And forgive them, as Jesus himself commands us: "Forgive, so your Father in heaven will forgive you" (Mark 11:25).

Childish questions about people's differences should be answered plainly, but mockery, disrespect, and derision should always be confronted; what starts as irreverence for other people can quickly turn into irreverence for God. For this reason, name-calling and teasing, as well as imitating another person's mannerisms or physical characteristics, should not be brushed off.

As for sexual sin, indecency should never be ignored, but harshness and moralism can cause great and even irreparable harm. Children go through periods of sexual curiosity, and we should never project our adult perversions onto them. They will ask questions about their bodies and about sex, which we should answer truthfully and without embarrassment – though without offering more information than they have asked for.

If a child offends in the sexual area, parents should appeal to the conscience, helping the child to choose right over wrong. Because a child will instinctively feel that what he has done is wrong, he may lie about it. Still, parents should be careful not to make too much of the matter; they should determine what actually took place, discipline the child, and then move on. Lengthy questioning and interrogation will only draw attention to the sexual area and burden the child even more.

My parents, who both worked as teachers, never tired of emphasizing what a great injustice it is to label children or adolescents for their misdeeds. They warned against drawing conclusions about a child's character and future development, and emphasized a constructive approach to help the child find new interests.

Given the bewildering array of child rearing methods that are promoted today, what good advice can parents trust? Benjamin Spock, whose books influenced an entire generation, suggested that parents know more than they think they know, and that they should trust their God-given instincts and abilities. To a degree, he was right: we need to trust our own judgment if we are to be effective parents. But there is more to parenthood than techniques and methods, and that is where God comes in. In searching for the best answers for their children, humble parents will always turn to him in prayer first.

To give children up as "hopeless" shows a lack of love and faith. If we truly love our children, we will never throw up our hands in despair. Even at the end of the roughest day, we cannot lose joy in them, and must believe that Christ's power to redeem and heal is there for them as much as it is for us.

19

Building Character

*Since we belong to the day, let us be self-controlled,
putting on faith and love as a breastplate,
and the hope of salvation as a helmet.*

---

1 Thessalonians 5:8

Building Character

We LIVE IN A TIME WHEN almost everything that our parents and grandparents taught us about God is scorned. This is seen most of all in public schools, where teachers increasingly fear teaching students what they really believe, and where faith has taken second seat to the modern gods of tolerance and neutrality.

Whereas teachers and pastors of past decades could openly champion the ideals of decency, hard work, and faith, those of us who promote the same values today risk being labeled as bigots – or charged with hate crimes. And the lengths to which fearful school boards and parents now go borders on the ridiculous: a teacher in California was recently censured for responding to a sneeze with the age-old "God bless you," and a high school in Rhode Island has been forced to cover over a gymnasium-wall prayer that exhorts students to honor their teachers and push their minds and hearts as well as their bodies.

As a speaker and writer who has worked in the field of conflict resolution for many years, I have addressed countless students at schools and high schools across New York City and its surroundings. I recently experienced this backlash myself at a suburban middle school, when I was asked to leave – midway through a morning assembly – because I brought God into the equation.

But how can we teach children anything sensible when we are told to leave God out? How can we ever teach values if we question the superiority of right over wrong, the brightness of light over darkness, or the warmth of love over hate?

There is a widespread feeling that if we stand up too strongly for our beliefs, we may hurt someone who does not share them. Certainly I do not espouse intolerance of other people's convictions or believe in forcing my own beliefs on others by buttonholing them. At the same time, I am sure that because so few of us have ever had to stand up for what we believe, we have become spineless. Not only our children, but we ourselves, lack the courage and conviction that come from being tested.

How can parents raise children with moral backbone – children who are able, as they grow up, to hold on to their convictions? First and foremost, we must instill in children a sense of moral courage, which is an attitude of confidence, determination, and perseverance. In his book *Freedom from Sinful Thoughts,* my father writes how a person's attitude to the difficulties he meets in life determines his emotional well-being. This is just as true for children. They must learn to adopt an aggressive attitude to cold, heat, and fatigue, and to apathy and indulgence, if they are ever to deal with fears, hurts, and disappointments.

Children need to learn to be plucky; they cannot dissolve in tears at every taunt or jeer. They must learn to withstand peer pressure and the humiliation of being despised for simply holding an unpopular idea. And they must realize that humility is no less vital to building character than the ability to think for oneself. It may take courage to hold an opposing viewpoint in a crowd, but it takes just as much courage, if not more, to own up to a mistake or to admit defeat when one is wrong.

Clearly, the formation of character only begins in childhood, and must continue as a lifelong process. Yet if parents lay a firm foundation for their children at home, they will not be disappointed. Friedrich Wilhelm

Foerster, a German writer and educator, says, "A child is educated not by having lengthy talks about 'big' things, but by patiently teaching him to carry out the smallest and most ordinary tasks properly. Character is formed through training in the smallest, mundane things – in the living room, and not in the stream of the world."

A child's strength of character (or lack of it) will have a bearing on his readiness to suffer for the sake of conviction. Given the measure of religious freedom we enjoy at present, some readers may find it strange to even raise this issue. Yet as someone who experienced the McCarthy era himself, I know that things can change quickly. Throughout history and right down to the present day, followers of almost every religion and ideology have had to endure opposition.

The sooner our children realize that discipleship means suffering and hardship, the better equipped they will be. I still remember a true story my parents told me as a child about the teenage son of a 16th century Austrian miller, who was executed because he refused to recant his "heretical" beliefs.

We should take care not to burden children with worrying about the future. At the same time it cannot hurt to make them think, even now, of how they might one day have to stand up for their beliefs.

Christoph Blumhardt wrote that his father spared no words when talking to his children about what this might mean:

> He gathered us regularly for prayer and Bible reading and spoke of the possible persecution that might be in store for those who confess the name of Jesus. I felt a thrill run through my whole body when at the end he exclaimed, with lively gestures, "Children, rather let your heads be cut off than deny Jesus!" Such an education awakened the good within me at an early age.

Jesus did not promise his followers good times. The greater our faith, the greater the opposition we may face because of it.

20

Consideration for Others

Do nothing out of selfish ambition or vain conceit,
but in humility consider others better than yourselves.
Each of you should look not only to your own
interests, but also to the interests of others.

Philippians 2:3–4

Consideration for Others

Name-calling and taunting have been around as long as there have been schools and children. Yet this problem has taken a new and sordid twist with the arrival of instant messaging and the Internet.

Cyber-bullying has become one of the most pernicious weapons in the hands of young teens today; many school resource officers tell me it is by far the worst form of bullying they have seen. It is perhaps so deadly because it works alone and in silence, and deeply damages a student's psyche.

Bullying is not just a social problem, either, but a medical one. Victims are now known to suffer post-traumatic stress syndrome, nightmares, over-eating, under-eating, and a greatly increased rate of suicide – especially in teen girls. And the effects of bullying at this formative age can last a lifetime; it is not just a harmless rite of passage or an inevitable part of growing up.

Bullying teens who are gay – or whom people *think* might be gay – is also a problem. Regardless of what we may feel about someone's lifestyle, it is never right to mistreat or marginalize someone simply because he is different. In fact, my father warned that "soul murder" is every bit as criminal as actual murder. It is precisely the teen who sticks out (or keeps to himself) who needs our love and positive encouragement. If we take the time and effort, we will always find common ground and a way to relate.

Hatred toward people of a different race, color, or culture is no different. It is also a learned thing; left to themselves, children will play happily together, oblivious of any differences in the shade of their skin. When they get older they will naturally begin to notice differences, yet even then their awareness will never be a matter of prejudice or hatred. Racism is present only among children whose self-awareness and awareness of others has been distorted by the adults around them.

Whenever any form of racism rears its head, we must point our children (and each other) away from the foolishness of human ideas about color, culture, and class. Most important, we must seek the love of God, who created us with all our differences, and show our children with words and deeds that we are committed to striving for justice and brotherhood among all men and women on earth.

It is relatively easy to raise children who are polite and who use good manners, but it is much harder to instill in them a genuine sensitivity to the perspectives and needs of others. True consideration is far more than a matter of manners. It means loving one's neighbor as oneself. It means seeing what is of God in another person.

There are many ways to encourage children in this way. They can buy flowers for a grandparent, bake cookies for a friend's birthday, or visit a lonely neighbor. And as they learn to see beyond their own small worlds, they will discover the satisfaction of bringing joy to others.

In his novel *The Brothers Karamazov*, Dostoevsky reminds us that the sensitivity of children is so great that we can shape their attitudes without even knowing it – and that our most effective lessons will be taught by example:

> Every day and hour, see that your image is a seemly one.
> You pass by a little child, you pass by, spiteful, with ugly
> words, with wrathful heart; you may not have noticed

the child, but he has seen you, and your image, unseemly and ignoble, may remain in his defenseless heart. You don't know it, but you may have sown an evil seed in him, and it may grow – all because you did not foster in yourself an active, actively benevolent love.

21

Teenagers

Similarly, encourage the young to be self-controlled.
In everything, set them an example
by doing what is good.

Titus 2:6–7

Teenagers

In a world which seems more rotten every day, it can be overwhelming to think of steering our children through the rocky years of adolescence. But if we have established a relationship of honesty and trust with our children early on, we will have firm ground on which to proceed, and it will be impossible for our children to resist us.

Many children slip easily through their early years, rearing their horns only once they are teens. But parents who hold back until there is conflict in the house may gain outward obedience only – and not the respect necessary to solve problems like lying, sexual impurity, mockery, and stealing.

Some young people simply will go through more difficult periods of development than others, and then we must be careful not to be too harsh and judgmental towards them. But even if we are big-hearted, we should not gloss over sin, especially when it involves sex. Sexual experimentation can scar young people for life, and we do them a disservice when we excuse it as "youthful indiscretion." All the more, young people who have sinned in this area must be led to repentance and to a conversion.

This can never be achieved through hard punishment – nor by persuasion or intellectual discussion. Rather, we must protect and nourish any flame of conscience that remains, even if it is small. My father always maintained that if a person followed his conscience, he could not go on living without bringing it in order. He compared the conscience to an Old Testament prophet. When the people of Israel went wrong, a prophet arose and called them back to God. When teens lie, steal, use drugs, get drunk, or have sex, the conscience in that child says, "This is wrong; now you have to be punished." The conscience demands action because God demands action. In other words, it is a guide – a rudder – and we must teach our children that it is not their enemy, but their best friend.

How to instill such a living conscience is no small thing. We must prepare the hearts of our children so that they become good soil for the Word of God. Preaching, however, does not make good soil; it hardens the heart. Still, all teenagers can understand that they are made in the image of God, and if they can see this as an obligation – as a calling, a task, and a responsibility – they can develop a self-discipline that will serve them in all areas. Those who learn to respect their bodies as temples will also be better equipped to resist the temptations of alcohol, drugs, or sex.

Like us, our children will still fail at one time or another, and then we must remember that just as God is not yet finished with them, he is not finished with us, either.

My own teenage years were difficult because my parents were often gone on long trips. What encouraged me then was to remember the stories about Jesus that my parents had told me when I was small. Later, my wife and I raised eight children of our own, who also went through rocky years. But it was the positive memories of our own childhood that gave us the courage to persevere and try to give a good childhood to them.

All of us want to pass on our values to the next generation, but we often fail to see that it is our actions, and not our words, that our children will carry with them – and that the only thing we can really pass on to our children is a living faith. Blumhardt, the nineteenth-century German pastor, lived in a time much more pious than ours, but still admonished parents who rushed their children to church: "As long as Christ lives only in your Bibles, and not in your hearts, every effort to bring him to your children will fail."

In many homes, a great deal of strife might be solved if parents were able to let go of their children and not fret over them, or pressure them with plans for their future. My mother, a teacher, used to tell parents, "The greatest disservice you can do your children is to chain them to yourselves. Let go of them!"

This advice can be hard to follow when our children are misbehaving – when they are rebelling and turning their backs on everything we have taught them. But just especially then, we have to pray rather than talk, and commit their souls to God. And we must take care not to pile too much blame upon ourselves, or to become bitter and despondent. Instead, we must believe. Saint Augustine lived a sinful life as a young man, but his mother, Monica, did not stop praying for him until he broke down and repented. Later he became a pillar of the church, and has influenced countless people in their search for God through the centuries.

Those who are tempted to dismiss an entire generation as dissolute or degenerate should stop and look at themselves: much as we hate to admit it, our children always mirror us. Parents today rightly wring their hands over texting and sexting, but then spend hours on their smartphones themselves; they are aghast at the sexually explicit material their sons and daughters are viewing but then leave pornographic magazines scattered around the house. There is no question that as parents, we can and should make rules about all of these things, but at the same time, we must also be good examples.

It is a privilege to lead young people to Jesus, to show them how marvelous God's world is despite the terrible impurity, corruption, and darkness of our age. And we can be comforted and encouraged along the way by the words of James: "Whoever turns a sinner from the error of his way will save him from death, and cover over a multitude of sins (Jas. 5:20).

22

Conclusion

For we are God's workmanship,
created in Christ Jesus to do good works,
which God prepared in advance for us to do.

Ephesians 2:10

Conclusion

It MUST BE WELL OVER eighty years ago that my grandfather stated that "every child is a thought of God." This means that we cannot and must not try to mold children according to our own ideas and wishes.

Few parents and educators even consider what God might have in mind for a particular child. But it is God, and not we, who created our children. He has a plan for each one, and our children will become themselves only if they are allowed to develop according to his will.

Too often, we think in human terms of success – about a sound and lucrative career or an honorable profession. We think we are doing our children a service by steering them in these directions, when in fact our meddling with God's plan risks harming their souls and stifling their inner growth.

Helping children discover their calling in life is perhaps the most difficult and challenging task we will ever face. Every child is unique, and even in the same family the differences between children can be astonishing. Yet if we listen to the advice Jesus gives us – to seek God's kingdom first, and to trust that everything else will then fall into place – we will not be disappointed.

My parents never pressed me or my sisters to pursue any particular field. Rather, they tried to awaken a social conscience in us – to feel the need of mankind. They also tried to instill in us a love for humanity – a compassion that embraced all of the masses, and which did not focus on the salvation of a select few.

We grew up during World War II and the suffering in Europe was constantly on our hearts and minds. In fact, we had no real chance for higher education, but our parents still insisted that we learn to work hard, both physically and mentally. They knew that this foundation would serve us well whatever we might end up doing.

My own hopes for the future changed continually. At first I wanted to be a farmer like my father, but he then befriended a lawyer and so I changed my mind. Later I thought about becoming a baker, or even a cowboy. In the end our family moved to the United States and I studied business. Even then, I remained in that field for only ten years before becoming a pastor.

Of course, all parents want their children to shine. They want credit for having done a good job of raising them. But we are mistaken if we measure people by their college degrees, salaries, or positions. God cares nothing for all of these things. He looks instead for souls that long to be close to him, and who yearn to spend their lives alleviating the misery and suffering of the people around them.

Bringing up children in this way requires constant prayer and attention. How do our children relate to others? Are they sociable and outgoing? Do they weep when others weep? And can they rejoice when others are happy?

Instead of pushing our children into the academic fast-track, we ought to teach them the prayer of Saint Francis, whose works are remembered almost 800 years after his death. It is this prayer that will save us, and save our children:

> Lord, make me an instrument of thy peace!
> Where there is hatred, let me sow love;

Where there is injury, pardon;
Where there is doubt, faith;
Where there is despair, hope;
Where there is darkness, light;
And where there is sadness, joy.

O divine Master –
Grant that I may not so much seek
To be consoled, as to console;
To be understood, as to understand;
To be loved, as to love.
For it is in giving that we receive,
In pardoning that we are pardoned,
And in dying that we are born to eternal life.

If you liked this book and want to talk more about children with others who care, visit www.WhyChildrenMatter.com

The Author

A NOTED SPEAKER and writer on the topics of marriage and family, education, and conflict resolution, Johann Christoph Arnold is a senior pastor at the Bruderhof Communities and also serves as chaplain for the local sheriff's department. He has traveled extensively and his books have been translated into more than 20 languages.

Born in 1940 to German refugees, he spent his boyhood years in South America, where his parents found asylum during the war; he immigrated to the United States in 1955.

He and his wife Verena have been married for 46 years. They have 8 children and 42 grandchildren, but feel that every child they meet is a grandchild.

Other books by Johann Christoph Arnold

Sex, God, and Marriage

Johann Christoph Arnold

Foreword by Mother Teresa

A marriage counselor for over forty years, Arnold addresses the pain resulting from broken relationships and the misuse of sexual intimacy. Fresh biblical insights on the sacredness of sex, the struggle against temptation, marriage, singleness, divorce, and much more.

Peter Kreeft *Boston College*
Clear, compassionate, uncompromisingly Christian...Pretty close, I think, to what Jesus would say if he were to write a book about sex today—and probably as socially acceptable as he was.

Pope Benedict XVI
I am very happy for this book and for its moral conviction. It will inevitably arouse hatred. But we must continue in trying to overcome evil with good.

To order or download a free e-book, visit: www.plough.com

Other books by Johann Christoph Arnold

Why Forgive?
Johann Christoph Arnold

Arnold avoids glib pronouncements by letting the untidy experiences of ordinary people speak for themselves. Here are people who have earned the right to talk about overcoming hurt, and who can tell of the peace they have found in doing so.

ALA Booklist, Starred Review
So powerful that tears often impede reading.

Houston Chronicle
Arnold writes with eye-opening simplicity that zings the heart.

Publishers Weekly
Noteworthy…profound and always timely…Arnold allows his subjects to speak for themselves. In all cases, he reminds us that to forgive is neither to excuse nor to anesthetize ourselves from the pain that attends life and love, but rather to enter again into life's fray.

To order or download a free e-book, visit: www.plough.com

Other books by Johann Christoph Arnold

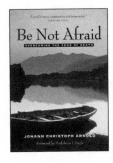

Be Not Afraid
Overcoming the Fear of Death
Johann Christoph Arnold
Foreword by Madeleine L'Engle

Fear of accidents, illness or dying, loneliness or grief – if you're like most people, such anxieties may be robbing you of the peace that could be yours. In *Be Not Afraid,* Arnold, a seasoned pastoral counselor who has accompanied many people to death's door, tells how ordinary people found the strength to conquer their deepest fears.

Paul Brand, M.D.
Author, *Pain: The Gift Nobody Wants*
I have read many books about dying, but this is the one I would give to someone dealing with death or facing grief. From start to finish it shines with hope. I want a copy beside my bed when my time comes.

To order or download a free e-book, visit: www.plough.com